MAKING
A HOUSE A
HOME

MAKING A HOUSE A HOME

Designing Your Interiors From the Floor Up

SUSANNA SALK

Principal photography by Stacey Bewkes

RIZZOLI
NEW YORK

New York Paris London Milan

Contents

Introduction

I've written about how to make a house more fearless, how to celebrate its little moments, and how to unleash the power of patterns within it. I've written about designers' primary homes as well as their weekend homes. I've even written about dogs sharing rooms with their designer owners. I've encouraged people over the years (I hope!) to be their own decorator through pages of varied visual inspiration. But after having written twelve design books, I have only now broken down what are a house's core elements, chapter by chapter, in hopes of helping you build—or rebuild—your own design from the ground up. This book, which brings you on a tour of some of the most beautiful rooms around the world, will help you do just that.

There's plenty to learn from these rooms—which are glorious in themselves—but the hope is that you will maybe cherry-pick an idea or two and apply it to an area in your house that needs rejuvenation. From floors to ceilings and everything in between, the designers share with us their very best practical instruction and inspiration. I hope the book is a place you will refer to time and time again for projects big *and* small.

As you page through, if something moves you, see if there's a way to translate it to your own home. But avoid taking it too literally. Have fun and don't worry. As you'll discover, the only "rule" that every design expert we featured can agree on is this: live only with what you love.

—Susanna Salk

Doors

A door is so much more than an entrance. It's your
house putting its best foot forward to welcome not
just visitors but *you*, its occupant, over and over again.
Make the most of it. Go beyond the holiday trim, and
instead consider its potential all year long. Consider
shape, hardware, and the surrounding landscape to
create an entrance that feels like a destination unto
itself. Stand in front of your door and imagine yourself
arriving for the very first time, waiting for it to
be opened. How does it make you feel? If you're not
delighted, then consider how best to change that.
If we all painted our front doors in our favorite color,
the world would surely be a brighter and happier place.

- Top left: A bright splash of color on a door is welcoming while also providing continuity to the interior space.

- Top right: Don't overlook the importance of hardware both as a design element and as a way to personalize your doors.

- Bottom left: If a door's placement is inconvenient in your space, you can always integrate it into the room's design.

- Bottom right: Above all, we want our entry doors to feel distinctive and substantial, as well as inviting.

Page 8: A door not only offers the opportunity to be a welcoming beacon for your return home, but it also provides a moment of surprise to anyone passing by. This blue-painted door on an old building is a powerful pop of color on a rainy day.

Opposite: Libertine cofounder Johnson Hartig frames his front door with layers of flora and fruit—not to mention color—to heighten the delicious sense of arrival.

Designed by Johnson Hartig

Above: Why not place your house number on a pair of sconces, as designer Nina Campbell does in her own London doorway? And while you're at it, why not paint your door a stunning bright blue and surround it with an arc of white roses?

Designed by Nina Campbell

Left: A wood door's very own material and detail can act as an elegant yet understated calling card, especially when juxtaposed against the texture of ivy.

Designed by Martin Lawrence Bullard

Above: Exterior doors can often be a style harbinger of what's to come. Here, designer Charlotte Barnes lets visitors know they are about to enter a world of sumptuous, refined color via the rich, glossy blue of her entrance.

Designed by Charlotte Barnes

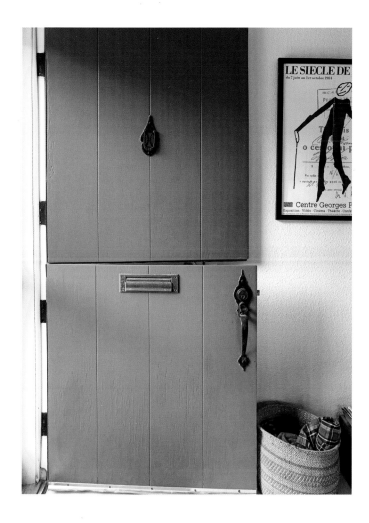

Opposite: In an upstairs landing of Robb Nestor and Bill Reynolds's River Road Farm, a door leading into a guest bedroom is painted in Benjamin Moore's high-gloss Palace Green, a favorite color of the owners that complements the toile on the chair pillow. The miniature chests on the shelves behind the door are salesman samples collected by Reynolds's family, who were in the furniture business.

Designed by Robb Nestor and Bill Reynolds

Above left: Isabelle Dahlin has always been obsessed with Dutch doors. "Even the back kitchen door is a smaller version of a Dutch door. Not only is it beautiful, it's really about the light. With only the top part open, it brings in great natural light. It feels secure but still inviting. I try to find vintage doors since they have character and history, but I have custom-made them for clients many times. Your front door is like your first impression, so it should be special."

Designed by Isabelle Dahlin

Above right: Never underestimate the power of an amazing door handle. Here, designer Charlotte Barnes pairs whimsical—and quite literal—handles in the shape of hands with an elegant white paint that makes the metal seem to glow with exotic elegance.

Designed by Charlotte Barnes

Below: A door is not just a way to block or allow access; it can also serve to frame whatever special objects await just beyond it. Make the most of every passageway by arranging wall color, artwork, and special objects with a sense of expectation for those who approach.

Designed by Edward Bulmer

Opposite: Designer Timothy Corrigan takes every opportunity to express his passion for French decorative arts in his Paris apartment. "The rooms, right down to the doors, retain all their historic detail, yet they still reflect my style, my needs, and my desires. To me, that is the definition of any successful decorating effort."

Designed by Timothy Corrigan

For the library in her converted barn, designer Emma Burns couldn't let the need for a door ruin the symmetry of the bookcases. "So it was a no-brainer to form a jib door within the run of joinery," she explains. "Everyone loves the idea of a secret door, and this also does a good job of providing great privacy to the bathroom on the other side."

Designed by Emma Burns

Opposite: "I love doors and find them a great opportunity for decoration," says Miles Redd. "Often it is an overlooked architectural feature that gets painted white and forgotten—but decorate your door, and you will see what it can do to your interiors." The ones that lead to his own office are a laser woodcut design inspired by fantasy pavilions and geometric patterns.

Designed by Miles Redd

Above: It's not always about the exterior door. Make the most of doors inside the home as well—like the one shown here that opens to a small bar— by painting them in a glamorous, glossy color.

Designed by Charlotte Barnes

"Green is the prevailing color at Hawthorne, our country home in the Hudson Valley," says Ted Kennedy Watson. "The green works so well as the house is set amongst the trees. We love that folks can drive by on the country road and get an instant hit of bright verdant green. In fact, we liked it so much that, after a bit, we painted the guesthouse front door the same green."

Designed by Ted Kennedy Watson and Theodore Sive

Windows

Windows don't just offer views, they supply character inside our rooms. They do this not just by their shapes but in the way they are framed. Whether they are dressed with bold, floor-length patterns or shades of soft solids or left bare to put functionality on view, windows are the eyes of your house with power as clear as the light they bring in.

- Top left: A small window can be treated as art, showcasing its unique shape as well as the nature outside.

- Top right: Bring the outdoors in with a floor-to-ceiling window, creating a wall of glass and light.

- Bottom left: Formal window treatments in an elegant pattern bring a cozy and comforting feeling to any space.

- Bottom right: Windows can serve as design elements, imparting character to a home through their distinct shapes, sizes, and colors.

Page 26: In Andrew Fisher and Jeffry Weisman's house in San Miguel de Allende, Mexico, this step-down guest bath shower area provided the unique opportunity to have a large window opening to the lushly planted patio. Since the opening is quite modern, the steel sash was divided to give it a scale more in keeping with the colonial architecture. The oval window at center pivots to bring in fresh air. The effect is modern but works with the architecture.

Designed by Andrew Fisher and Jeffry Weisman

Opposite: "When I devised the overall plan for my living room, I knew I wanted a beautiful table as part of a generous scheme," says designer Suzanne Rheinstein of the Montecito house she fashioned from scratch. "This light-filled corner is wonderful for looking at picture books, playing card games with my granddaughters, and for intimate lunches and dinners with a friend or two. It is always gracious to have a place for hors d'oeuvres when serving a larger group."

Designed by Suzanne Rheinstein

Opposite: Designers Bruce Glickman and Wilson Henley replaced the windows of their 1930s gabled cottage with ones made of restoration glass that are manufactured to have a wavy or antiqued look. By doing this, the designers could update the house while maintaining its nostalgic charm.

Designed by Wilson Henley and Bruce Glickman

Above left: This 1668 home in Locust Valley, New York, proves that the size, placement, and correlation between shutters and windows sets the distinct tone of a house before you even cross its threshold.

Designed by Jeffrey Bilhuber

Above right: Designer Mark D. Sikes knows that making a first impression is everything when it comes to your home's exterior. To that end, he used ivy and low hedges to gracefully mirror the shape of the windows and arched entry. The result is not only visually seamless but warm and beckoning.

Designed by Mark D. Sikes

Windows don't just act as frames in and of themselves in homes—they, too, can be framed. On the exterior of their Ojai home, designers Brooke and Steve Giannetti planted ivy and added potted fruit trees to accentuate the special panes of an exterior door that leads into their dining room.

Designed by Brooke and Steve Giannetti, Giannetti Home

Classically proportioned steel-sash French doors suit the scale and colonial style of designers Andrew Fisher and Jeffry Weisman's Mexico retreat.

Designed by Andrew Fisher and Jeffry Weisman

Above: In a half-Tudor, half-19th-century house, a little window can make a big impact when its simple presence is offset by beams and fresh white paint.

Designed by Paolo Moschino and Philip Vergeylen

Opposite: Windows aren't just about letting light in: using distinct shapes, sizes, and colors can add personality throughout a house or subtly carry a theme, like this star-shaped window in the Nantucket cottage shared by designers Gary McBournie and William Richards.

Designed by Gary McBournie and William Richards

Left: In Mexico, a bronze lantern sculpted by Andrew Fisher, with a handblown glass form covering the light, dangles like jewelry. The oval opening in the wall was created to bring daylight to the short stair to the living room.

Designed by Andrew Fisher and Jeffry Weisman

Below: To still be close to her animals and herb garden even while she works, designer Brooke Giannetti installed glass windows and doors all along one side of her Ojai office walls.

Designed by Brooke and Steve Giannetti, Giannetti Home

"Since this room is essentially covered in beadboard, I wanted to have a patterned fabric to create a bit of warmth and interest," says designer Charlotte Barnes. "So I added a trim on the shades and on the leading edge of the curtains to set off the color and pattern."

Designed by Charlotte Barnes

Above left: Nobody understands how to casually drape a country window better than the English. Sophie Conran accentuates the window's large proportions without detracting from the extensive gardens just outside.

Designed by Sophie Conran

Above right and opposite: Window curtains and trim are one of the most important and inventive ways to accessorize a room. Not only do they complete the architectural frame of the window, but they also offer a contained yet impactful way to add color and a dash of pattern and texture to nearby adjacent walls.

Designed by Charlotte Barnes

Opposite: "Steve and I loved the idea of an outdoor shower, but the mild Ojai weather wasn't predictable enough to pull it off," says Brooke Giannetti. "So we did the next best thing in our bathroom: We created a glassed-in shower that connects us to our garden. The sycamore trees and the Boston ivy provide shade in the summer; in the winter, the trees and vines lose their leaves, allowing the sun to warm the room."

Designed by Brooke and Steve Giannetti, Giannetti Home

Below: A window brings a dash of delight to a bathroom. Colorful tile always feels cheerful.

Designed by Andrew Fisher and Jeffry Weisman

Walls

Wallpapered, painted, covered with art or left bare, walls give a room's décor an invaluable visual layer. How they each correspond to one another is much like orchestrating a good dinner party: there needs to be diversity, glamour, character, and chicness. Edit your walls as much as you fill them. They should never overwhelm the room but always enhance it.

- Top left: By using the same pattern on the walls as on the curtains, you can create an elegant enveloping impact in your space.

- Top right: A richly colorful coat of paint on the walls is an inexpensive, yet lavish, way to bring a distinctive flair to a room.

- Bottom left: Have fun when showcasing your artworks. Displaying an art collection on a patterned background elevates it and creates a compelling vignette.

- Bottom right: A handsome painting hung at eye level camouflages an uneven wall, bringing beauty and drama to the space.

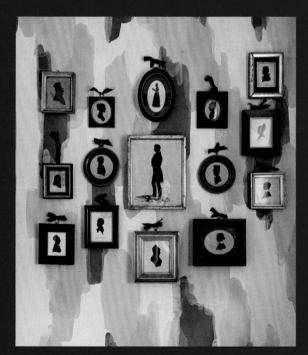

Page 44: In her London abode, designer Lulu Lytle layers exotic elements from her global travels and concocts a seating area that is uniquely her own. Her bold yet unpretentiously patterned wall sets the pitch-perfect tone.

Designed by Lulu Lytle

Right: A Lee Jofa chintz envelops the drawing room in Veere Grenney's Tangier home. By continuing the pattern on the curtains, the designer ensures that its elegant impact is unbroken. On the sofas, soft-hued solids—from his own linen collection— serve as a grounding influence to the strong floral pattern.

Designed by Veere Grenney

"These walls in my bedroom are tactile and materially complex," says Caleb Anderson. "They are layered with texture, color, and dimension. Here, the moiré envelops the room in a tranquil motion that has a calming quality reminiscent of water. The ceramic art installation adds unexpected visual interest, organically moving from one material to the next. With any dark room, contrast is key—the white shades on the girandole lamps, flowers, and objects appear bolder against the deep blue backdrop."

Designed by Caleb Anderson

Opposite: In Caleb Anderson's study, the hand-painted wallcovering on a metallic gold ground glows between citrine-colored moldings. The repetitive use of golds and yellows imbues a warmth and solar energy to the room, all of which is reflected in the depth of the handcrafted paper. The walls hold their own here, while providing a complementary back-drop to the large painting, antique clock.

Designed by Caleb Anderson

Below: Wallpaper with an oversize pattern can open up the boundaries and possibilities of a room in magical ways. This hand-painted silk wall covering by Fromental, Bruyère, proves that patterns don't always have to repeat themselves to have an impact.

Arranged by Beth Dempsey of Images and Details

For London designer Alidad, wall color isn't just a backdrop, but instead a star player. In this passageway, the designer uses opulent reds and golds to sumptuously set the mood for his entire home. The color also extends to the jib door—hidden at the far end of the hall—that disguises a bathroom.

Designed by Alidad

"Sometimes you find the perfect space you have been collecting for all along," says designer Thomas O'Brien, describing the stair hall of his home in the country. He had been collecting Impressionist landscapes for many years and finally decided that this entryway was the perfect place to display them. "Some are very special and were acquired at auction, while others weren't more than a hundred dollars," says O'Brien. The designer framed them and then chose a pale pink-and-silver chinoiserie wallpaper as a backdrop. Displayed together in this way, says O'Brien, "they have long-lasting meaning."

Designed by Thomas O'Brien

Below: A staircase need not be grand to get a grand treatment. For the stair hall of her Millbrook, New York, house, designer Katie Ridder designed her own sgraffito-inspired wall covering—called Scraffito—after being inspired on a trip to Prague.

Designed by Katie Ridder

Opposite: Using different tones of a single color can result in a delightful interplay of wall and furnishings. For example, in her New York City library, Bunny Williams covered the wall in Penny Morrison's soft green Tulkan and juxtaposed it with the John Sofa from her home line upholstered in a mossy green fabric. The textural bookcase, also in a green tone, along with the dark green velvet cushions on the tapestry chair, all tie into the chic theme.

Designed by Bunny Williams

Above: Big rooms with expansive walls can have their dimensions accentuated by displaying a collection evenly over their entire surface. In a guesthouse on the grounds of their Sussex farmhouse, designers Paolo Moschino and Philip Vergeylen placed a collection of white-framed vintage maps against the white walls in groups of three, creating an elegantly streamlined, rather than cluttered, effect.

Designed by Paolo Moschino and Philip Vergeylen

Opposite: In her Oxfordshire manor, designer Bridget Elworthy finds a creative solution to this room's special architecture. For this odd space between raised pillars, the designer allows it to shine by adding the perfect-size painting and then accenting with accessories that further elevate it.

Designed by Bridget Elworthy

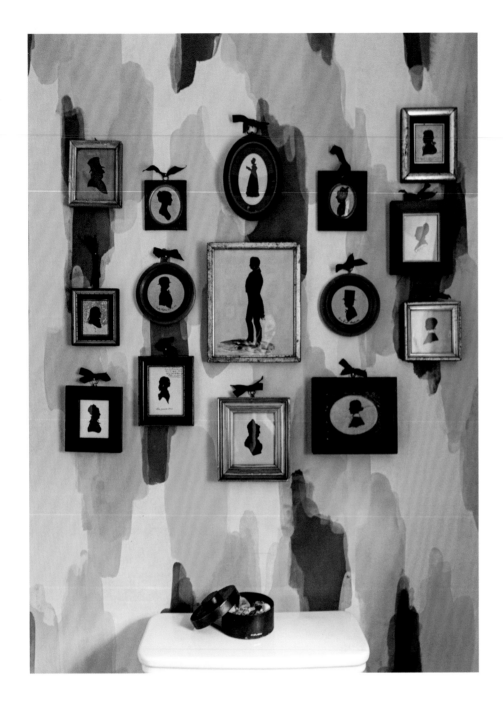

Guest bathrooms are a wonderful place to have fun and experiment, where the smaller scale offers ways to get creative without a big commitment. Here, in her own guest bathroom, Kate Brodsky elevates her collection of traditional silhouettes with a uniquely abstract wallpaper pattern that picks up on the colors of the frames.

Designed by Kate Brodsky

"We were drawn to creating a room that had personality but was at the same time relaxing," says Maximilian Sinsteden of the room he and his designer partner, Catherine Casteel Olasky, created for the Kips Bay Decorator Show House. "We felt putting the pattern on the walls—as opposed to the more conventional method of putting it on the curtains—would give the room an enveloping feeling. This green leaf print felt traditional, with an edge of modernity. To us, the layers are what make interiors possible, and in this room the patterned walls are the basis for it all."

Designed by Olasky & Sinsteden

Below: "Henri Samuel's blue-and-white room for [novelist] Louise de Vilmorin was the inspiration for my bedroom," says Emily Evans Eerdmans. "The shared DNA of delftware color palette and chinoiserie decoration makes the layering of patterns work."

Designed by Emily Evans Eerdmans

Opposite: Designer Isabelle Dahlin isn't afraid of having fun with pattern. In a guest room of her Ojai house, she shows how patterned walls can interplay with bed linens in casually festive ways.

Designed by Isabelle Dahlin

Opposite: In his Tangier bedroom, designer Nicolò Castellini Baldissera continues his love affair with color, proving that the power of deep, sumptuous color on walls knows no limits.

Designed by Nicolò Castellini Baldissera

Above: In her girls' room, Kate Brodsky calibrates the cheery patterned wallpaper with everything in the room, while still leaving space for playfulness. The flowers on the wallpaper seem to have wafted across the room to lightly settle on the surface of the bed linens.

Designed by Kate Brodsky

Above left: In the seating area of designers Frank de Biasi and Gene Meyer's Tangier bedroom, beige stripes add a lively tone while still making the space feel calm.

Designed by Frank de Biasi and Gene Meyer

Above right: Glimpses of a colorful patterned wallpaper set off the wonderful jewel and gold tones of designer Charlotte Barnes's glassware, becoming a delightful— and surprising—design element.

Designed by Charlotte Barnes

Opposite: A wall in designer Thomas O'Brien's study is upholstered in a favorite fabric called Nympheus, one he has often used for his clients. "It's a block pattern of a lily pond from Lee Jofa. For myself I used the reverse, which I always found beautiful in its abstract nature," says O'Brien, who recolored the block pattern in an eggplant colorway. "I love how the natural pattern surrounds the windows looking out to parts of the garden."

Designed by Thomas O'Brien

Floors

Our floors literally ground us, so what we do with them, in turn, grounds the room visually. A room's furniture can only look as balanced and vibrant as the floor beneath it, so the scale and tone of your carpet is crucial. But don't be *too* careful. Be bold rather than bland. Do a bit of the unexpected on each surface, even if it means going bare and letting the floor's very essence speak for itself.

◆ Top left: If you prefer to avoid rugs, painting a custom pattern is an elegant and simple treatment for your bare floor.

◆ Top right: A staircase is the perfect place to show off a distinctive rug.

◆ Bottom left: A shiny and colorful painted floor is a cheerful and creative way to personalize your kitchen.

◆ Bottom right: If your house doesn't come with terrazzo floors, you can create them, imparting an Italian flair to your kitchen.

Page 68: "Color on the floor is a neat idea if you feel it's something you can live with forever, and we do," says designer Katie Ridder of the purple-tiled entry hall in the home she shares with her husband, architect Peter Pennoyer. "I then painted the surrounding walls a neutral color to balance it out. In Europe you see patterned and colored tiles on the floor all over."

Designed by Katie Ridder and Peter Pennoyer

Opposite: "I have geometric painted floors in several rooms in three houses," says Carolyne Roehm. "It's a great solution if the quality of the wooden floors is not good. It also works well if the space is dark or small—painting a design on the floor can change the visual effect dramatically. And painted borders can really define a space."

Designed by Carolyne Roehm

Opposite: For the entry of her Connecticut house, Bunny Williams stenciled a parquet floor over the antique pinewood boards. The design is not only practical to clean—think muddy paw prints—but the effect is as visually pleasing as a rug pattern.

Designed by Bunny Williams

Above: "Painted floors have been around for centuries," says designer Heather Chaddock. "This graphic pattern brings character to the mudroom and the distressed technique makes the floor look as if it's been here for one hundred years!"

Designed by Heather Chaddock Interiors

Page 76: Classic black-and-white floors make a big impact in this chic farmhouse laundry room.

Designed by Heather Chaddock Interiors

Page 77: "I love a painted floor in a bedroom, especially as I am mostly barefooted here," says designer Bunny Williams. "I wanted a light floor and chose the gray pattern to complement the mirrored bed. Gray and pink is a favorite combination of mine."

Designed by Bunny Williams

Opposite: A floor doesn't have to let the rest of the room be the star of the show. Here, the flooring in Nicolò Castellini Baldissera's Tangier bedroom more than holds its own amid the colorful walls, bed frame, linens, and patterned rug. Everything works together in an unstudied way, creating a stylish spontaneity that feels deeply personal.

Designed by Nicolò Castellini Baldissera

Above left: "Painted floors are an old-time Yankee tradition, and this orange-and-white checkerboard floor is our way to bring the tradition forward," says designer Gary McBournie. In this New England house, orange and white squares were placed on the diagonal to give the illusion of a wider space.

Designed by Gary McBournie and William Richards

Above right: "Terrazzo has always been a passion of mine," says designer Bunny Williams, "especially whenever I see the large chunks of marble in Italian churches and palazzos. I knew I wanted this same design feeling for our own Manhattan kitchen, and when I found that I could make this, I was thrilled."

Designed by Bunny Williams

Opposite: A floor's pattern can be the ideal backdrop for your dining room chairs. In his Connecticut dining room, designer Robert Couturier effortlessly complemented a classic black-and-white diamond design floor with chairs upholstered in a bold red velvet. The sheer curtains carry the theme with subtle red accents.

Designed by Robert Couturier

Below: A staircase need not just be a boring passageway. Here, Emma Burns, design director of Sibyl Colefax & John Fowler, proves that point by cleverly enlivening a pedestrian stairway by covering it with a vintage rug.

Designed by Emma Burns, Sibyl Colefax & John Fowler

Opposite: Designer Gavin Houghton loves the classic Moroccan chevron motif so much that he re-created it here for the floor of his Tangier terrace. "Green and white is a favorite color combination of mine," says Houghton.

Designed by Gavin Houghton

Living Rooms

As many of us live so much in our kitchen and home offices now, what happens to the room whose name supposedly sums up the very nature of home? It's simple: we can honor it by making it a seamless part of the flow of other spaces and by distinguishing it with a décor that invites us to sit, relax, and engage with one another. A living room should feel edited but not overly pared down. It should have dignity without being formal. All of its elements must be in sync without its layout feeling too predictable. Living rooms should feel lively and, ultimately, *lived* in.

- Top left: Your living room serves many functions—it's a place for entertaining, as well as a place to relax after a long day—so it needs to be welcoming and reflect your personal style.

- Top right: A soothing and sophisticated neutral palette emphasizing texture and clean lines.

- Bottom left: Creating different seating areas to take advantage of a built-in library or to enjoy the views out the window ensures that all of the space is well used.

- Bottom right: A large, stunning artwork can serve as a needed focal point in a room filled with a variety of treasures.

Page 84: "Painting trim and cabinetry the same color as the walls is a favorite thing for me," says designer Katie Ridder. "It simplifies the space. This room in our home is used a lot: it's tucked away, and it's small, like a cocoon."

Designed by Katie Ridder and
Peter Pennoyer

Pages 88-89: "My house in Santa Barbara is small, charming, and historic," says designer Madeline Stuart of her 1930s one-bedroom weekend house in a historic neighborhood. "I sought to create an environment that's comfortable, conducive to casual evenings with friends, and relatively dog-proof for our two Parson Russell terriers. To that end, I mixed vintage finds, Spanish antiques, comfortable upholstery, and far too many accessories!"

Designed by Madeline Stuart

Opposite: In his Manhattan living room, John Derian, owner of the famous shop that bears his name, enjoys creating multiple seating areas. "I like being able to use the room in different ways and to enjoy the different views," he says. "This nook is a perfect spot." A generous spray of branches links the indoors with the out and adds succulent color to the creamy undertones of the surrounding décor.

Designed by John Derian

"I'd always wanted to do a classic interior contrasted with the modern city views outside, and I got my wish with our apartment in New York," says Frank de Biasi. "As always, Gene and I experimented with new ideas, here using his wallpaper for Holland & Sherry as a neutral backdrop. Our furniture was repurposed from our old house in Miami, so there is a bit of Oliver Messel tropical influence with the printed fabrics and fresh colors."

Designed by Frank de Biasi and Gene Meyer

Pages 94-95: In the salon of his country home, designer Veere Grenney highlighted the unique details of the ceiling by painting the wall in a pale pink that unifies the whole while still articulating the room's special layers.

Designed by Veere Grenney

Opposite: When it comes to using unexpected colors in familiar places, designer Miles Redd relies on his instincts. "Trust your gut," says Redd, who did just that in his Manhattan living room before adding layers of favorite objects and mementos. "When I showed friends I was going to do a pink-and-red room, I definitely got some raised eyebrows, but I am a collector by nature, and I knew certain elements would bring it down a bit. I did this almost 25 years ago, and am still happy with the results, which is all that matters."

Designed by Miles Redd

In his Paris apartment, designer
Timothy Corrigan cleverly
solved the impracticality of
having six pairs of doors in his
living room by removing one,
setting an antiqued mirror panel
into another, and disguising the
other four by placing consoles,
mirrors, and paintings in front
of them, with the ornate plaster-
work serving as frames. As a
result, the room is comforting
and hospitable rather than
feeling like a passageway.

Designed by Timothy Corrigan

"My home is a celebration of the world's diverse and splendid cultures, collected during a lifetime of travel," says Susan Walker, founder of Ibu Movement. "A geometric-pattern phulkari embroidered in the Punjab brightens the settee, as do cushions made from vintage saris. A colorful child's hat from Rajasthan, altar vessels from Thailand, a santos from Guatemala, inlaid tables from Fez, Morocco, beaded betel-lime containers from Timor, and a ceramic bowl found in Japan all live in peace and make for a livelier whole. I enter the room in conversation with the world."

Designed by Susan Walker

Creating a classic seating area doesn't necessarily mean getting locked into some traditional formula. In the salon of their upstate New York farmhouse, Karen Suen-Cooper and Martin Cooper's unexpected choice of the orange wall color and pattern and surrounding darker trim immediately distinguishes this room. The pairing of Regency-style armchairs with more modern pieces reflects their lives and passions in an edited yet carefree manner.

Designed by Karen Suen-Cooper and Martin Cooper for the Punctilious Mr. P's Place Card Co.

"I believe in the power of texture, art, and accessories to unify a room and also distinguish it," says designer Tamara Meadow Bernstein. Her Connecticut lake house for her family is a glamorous and comfortable haven because of this philosophy.

Designed by Tamara Meadow Bernstein

Opposite: "I created a corner near this window where I could read or sit and chat with a friend," says designer Bunny Williams of this stylish nook in her Manhattan living room. Her salon-style way of displaying art accentuates the space, and the beautiful textiles of the throw and pillows further beckon you to the sofa.

Designed by Bunny Williams

Above: "Combining antiques and classical elements with contemporary pieces is a design vernacular I have become very confident with," says designer Caleb Anderson. "In my own Manhattan living room, a classical urn is situated next to bold contemporary artwork and an antique gilt bergère is nestled next to a midcentury-style sofa. Swooping curves in the artwork, custom rug, and coffee table bring the room together in a dynamic fashion."

Designed by Caleb Anderson

"Our Tangier living room was created from scratch, which was fortunate, as I'd always wanted a room with windows on all sides," says Frank de Biasi of the Tangier home he created with partner Gene Meyer. "The colors I used come from the plants on the terraces. I wanted a touch of North Africa, which we have in the Mauretanian straw-and-leather mat on the floor and with the two small painted low tables in the foreground."

Designed by Frank de Biasi and Gene Meyer

In his Locust Valley, New York, weekend house, designer Jeffrey Bilhuber deftly mixed bold colors, prints, and patterns to prove that a living room need not be visually quiet to be graciously elegant.

Designed by Jeffrey Bilhuber

Ceilings

Ceilings are often called the fifth wall, but they are the first line of defense when it comes to protecting your world within. They can also unexpectedly define a room's mood, so their power should not be under-estimated. Whether you decide to highlight them with a distinct color or allow them to blend in with the walls, they can lift the space and your spirits instantly.

- Top left: The simple lines of the arched ceiling envelop this indoor/outdoor space and help keep it cool during the heat of summer.

- Top right: The high arched ceiling and exposed wood beams, with the addition of ceiling fans, complement the wooden display shelves and bring a tropical, airy vibe to this great room.

- Bottom left: You can instantly transform the room's architecture by tenting the ceiling or swathing it in fabric, creating a completely different feeling for the space.

- Bottom right: If your ceiling doesn't have a beautiful medallion molding, you can always create one and add an antique pendant for historical grandeur.

Page 112: Adding a faux architectural detail is one way to bring structure and visual interest to an otherwise blah room. For example, the ceiling coffers on designer Alexa Hampton's bedroom are "entirely without functional use," she says. "I installed them to bring geometric rigor and architectural interest to my small bedroom that had neither. Finally, the plaster moldings and center medallion give a nod to historic design and add no small amount of glamour. Perhaps it is the actual non-utility of these details that make me feel so very spoiled."

Designed by Alexa Hampton

Right: Martin Cooper and Karen Suen-Cooper go for fearless color in their black dining room, including painting the ceiling. "It cocoons the room," says Martin. Mirrors create reflective surfaces and the illusion of expanded space. "Keep your tablescapes simple," he adds. "Always bring a bit of the outdoors to your table. And consider adding dimmers to all electric lights, so they can be dialed up or down, then blend as much real candlelight in as you can."

Designed by Karen Suen-Cooper and Martin Cooper for The Punctilious Mr. P's Place Card Co.

Opposite: In his Tangier home, designer Gavin Houghton brings a sense of play to a seating area, perfectly proving the point that the ceiling is the fifth wall. "The striped fabric was woven for me in Tangier first," says Houghton. "The striped ceiling came about because I love the white walls in Morocco but wanted some fun. I now have clients that request it once they see it."

Designed by Gavin Houghton

Above: Using your imagination to expand your ceiling's horizon can result in a room brimming with timeless elegance. Here, Michael Trapp brings his wanderlust to his 19th-century guesthouse in Connecticut by tenting the room with a gold 18th-century fabric.

Designed by Michael Trapp

"The proverbial 'silk purse out of a sow's ear' saying holds true in the case of this tricky guest bedroom," says designer Jeffrey Bilhuber. "The sloped ceiling was a given and had to be addressed. There was no camouflaging it. So I decided it's best to embrace these obstacles and turn them into opportunities. The decorative tape trim on the walls carries up onto the ceiling to add architecture and structure. When you're in bed, there's only one way to look, and that's straight up, so it's best to make the most of it."

Designed by Jeffrey Bilhuber

Below: In their Ojai, California, home, design team Brooke and Steve Giannetti's arched ceilings heighten the sense of passage from indoors to outdoors and then back again while making it feel seamless.

Designed by Brooke and Steve Giannetti, Giannetti Home

Opposite: The great room of designer Richard Mishaan's 16th-century Cartagena house—from the carved and painted ceiling to the plaster walls painted with a chalk paint—was restored to its original state. The wall-size built-in bookshelf is filled with artifacts, along with contemporary art and objects, that tell the story of the house's history.

Designed by Richard Mishaan

"Our dining room is a series of contradictions that make the space feel special," says designer Bruce Glickman of the Connecticut space in which he and his partner, Wilson Henley, regularly entertain. "We installed a rustic ceiling made of antique lumber above a highly lacquered midcentury burl table with a chrome base. The plaster-covered brass chandelier feels both modern and traditional. The well-worn Moroccan Tuareg mat, with its geometric design, is surrounded by sleek modern art, which we love, even without walls to hang it all on."

Designed by Bruce Glickman and Wilson Henley

Opposite: "Laylights (ceiling windows that allow light to filter to lower levels) are a feature of many of our house projects," says designer Katie Ridder of the celestial ceiling in the home she shares with her husband, architect Peter Pennoyer. "Our inspiration for this radial pattern of custom-colored stars came from the tradition of domes. The stars are arranged in circles on the flat, translucent glass. They fade from red to pale orange, suggesting a curved plane."

Designed by Katie Ridder and Peter Pennoyer

Above: While restoring Staats Hall, his 1839 weekend house in Red Hook, New York, photographer Pieter Estersohn wanted to remain as true as possible to its Greek Revival roots: "This is a big room and needed the medallions to fit the monumental scale of the space."

Designed by Pieter Estersohn

Garrow Kedigian created this chalkboard lounge (an ode to Napoleon's love for worldly collections) for the Kips Bay Show House. Proceeds from the show house fund programs for children so "what better way to inspire children about design than to use a medium that they can relate to?" says Kedigian. "And what better medium than chalk? I decided to create a formal architectural language rendered in chalk. The walls were not sprayed to affix the chalk work. It was part of the fun watching people's reactions as they reached out to rub the white panel lines!"

Designed by Garrow Kedigian

Above: Renowned floral artist and entertaining maven Cathy Graham designed the shelves in her Nantucket flower room to exhibit the beautiful bottles she uses for arrangements she creates with blooms straight from her garden. "With its white walls, deep sink, high worktable, and stone floor, it is the perfect flower room," effuses Graham.

Designed by Cathy Graham

Opposite: "We wanted to treat this open porch as an outdoor dining and living room, and to bring the indoors outside," says William Richards of the Nantucket porch he shares with his partner, Gary McBournie. "The pair of bell jar lights suggests just a touch of formality."

Designed by Gary McBournie and William Richards

Dining Rooms

The dining room has been downgraded over the past decade as a "pass-by" room. But as of late, especially in this new age of "work from home," we need a separate space whose site-specific function is a call to action: gather, be seated, and share a meal. And a dining room's design needn't be limited to the functional: bursts of color, whimsical lighting, and unexpected curves in the chairs or table offer a rich feast for the eyes.

- Top left: Painting the walls and shelves in the same muted shade allows the displayed china collections and patterned tablecloth and drapes to coexist elegantly without looking fussy.

- Top right: With its enveloping blue-and-white wallpaper and rug, the textured blue ceiling and fantasy chandelier, and a cheerful orange dining set, this oasis is a perfect example of going bold with your dining room.

- Bottom left: With its facing mirrors and large crystal chandelier, this black-painted dining room sparkles with sophistication.

- Bottom right: This serene dining room is created from a neutral palette of natural materials with floor-to-ceiling windows that bring in light and nature.

Page 132: "Even your morning granola deserves a grand space!" says designer and potter Jonathan Adler. "For our Manhattan dining room, I serve glamour along with a graphic rug, persimmon-velvet chairs, and gold window treatments that accentuate the dining room's double-height ceiling. It's impossible to have a bad day when you start it off in a space that's as sunny, colorful, and glamorous as you are."

Designed by Jonathan Adler

Pages 136-137: A dining room doesn't necessarily need a carpet to feel company-worthy. To get a comparable feel, designer Kate Brodsky painted her floor a verdant green throughout. The hand-painted garden mural above the wainscoting makes it feel like you are sitting in a pergola on a gorgeous summer day.

Designed by Kate Brodsky

Opposite: With its lacquered red walls and gold accents, designer Caleb Anderson's small Manhattan dining room is a dramatic jewel box oozing glamour. Antique gold mirrors installed in a cubist pattern on the walls and the ceiling add shimmer. The table itself is veined golden spider marble flanked by a banquette upholstered in red velvet and red-and-gold chairs. The dazzling 1920s Baccarat chandelier is reflected to infinity, amplifying the sparkle in this windowless room. "Dining rooms can always be an opportunity to wow and create an unforgettable dinner party experience," says Anderson.

Designed by Caleb Anderson

Page 140: This dining room was designed around an 18th-century French screen that designers Paolo Moschino and Philip Vergeylen bought at Christie's in Paris. They complemented it with their collection of antique blue-and-white delft on the walls. But when the room was finished, it looked unbalanced, so they called on specialist painter Dawn Reader to reproduce a tree from the screen's design on the two other walls. "Now," says Moschino, "we have dinner in a blue-and-white forest!"

Designed by Paolo Moschino and Philip Vergeylen

Above: In his 17th-century house, designer Carlos Sánchez-García wanted to reflect its old spirit without being too orthodox. The tapestry in the dining room not only reflects this period but adds texture and depth. "I didn't want the tapestry to be the focal point in the room," says Sánchez-García, "so I placed furniture in front of it. I find the marriage of delftware, tapestry, and oak one of the most infallible decoration tricks." The space is entirely lit by candlelight via a 17th-century Flemish chandelier and candle wall sconces.

Designed by Carlos Sánchez-García

Pages 142-143: A digital wall print of a John Constable painting dreamily expands the proportions of designer Justin Van Breda's Cotswolds dining room. Glass globes hanging from a tree branch (cut from his garden and attached to the ceiling beam) seem to float in midair. The combination of the natural and the fabricated—the real and the faux—suspends the senses and invites you to sit down and wonder.

Designed by Justin Van Breda

Above: In West Sussex, designers Paolo Moschino and Philip Vergeylen created an evergreen garden that can be enjoyed throughout the year. By building an extension off the kitchen with its own sitting area, they can enjoy the view even on cold days. "With the large window," says Vergeylen, "we feel as if we're always in the garden."

Designed by Paolo Moschino and Philip Vergeylen

Opposite: A cheerfully patterned tablecloth and slip-cover soften the imposing proportions of designer Penny Morrison's dining table, making it feel cozy instead of formal. "This was originally the laundry room of the house, so we added the bookcases, panels, and fireplace and painted everything in the room the same color," says Morrison. "The shelves were the perfect place for my chintz jug collection. It is a sunny room with a conservatory feeling and perfect for using our fresh summery tablecloths and plates!"

Designed by Penny Morrison

Left: Wood paneling is a perfect backdrop for a series of botanical prints that give warmth and a focal point to this large dining room in the English countryside. The lightly striped curtains, the white linens draped in a casual manner, and the sisal floor covering ensure that the room's grand proportions feel neither fussy nor unwelcoming.

Designed by Bridget Elworthy

Above: "Our London dining room is rather theatrical," says designer Philip Vergeylen. "But this is on purpose. It's certainly not to impress but rather to amuse and to make dinners with our guests feel special. Interestingly, this room started off as the worst possible space in that everything was in the wrong location. So we centered the entrance door and added a fake door on the opposite wall to balance it."

Designed by Paolo Moschino and Philip Vergeylen

"My dining room is a wonderful, classical shape with perfect Regency proportions," says designer Sophie Conran. "It has three floor-to-ceiling windows that flood it with light and provide amazing views of the countryside. I wanted to enhance this wonderful room, to make it a perfect place to enjoy the company of friends and family."

Designed by Sophie Conran

Below: In a restored Sussex barn, Paolo Moschino and Philip Vergeylen created a guesthouse that is at once dramatic and inviting. "We kept all original beams exposed, and they create an interesting web that showcases the building of the roof," says Moschino.

Designed by Paolo Moschino and Philip Vergeylen

Opposite: Designers Robb Nestor and Bill Reynolds's outdoor dining area, known as "The Temple," is dedicated to the four seasons but is also a favorite spot for summer dinners. "We love to light it by candlelight," says Nestor, "and fill it with plants and antique family wicker." Here, the couple set their charming table with a tablecloth and matching linens from Creel and Gow, Christopher Spitzmiller china, and glassware from William Yeoward.

Designed by Robb Nestor and Bill Reynolds

Johnson Hartig is fearless when it comes to his breakfast nook, which he affectionately dubbed "The Grotto Room." He sponge-painted the trims and ceiling to give the room a unified look and then covered its walls with his Plates and Platters wallpaper pattern for F. Schumacher to further intensify the blue-and-white experience. The chandelier enhances the whimsical timelessness of the space.

Designed by Johnson Hartig

Quintessence blog founder Stacey Bewkes brought the world home to her island cottage with a tablecloth from India, plates from France, and napkins from Portugal. "I love how my unusual shell collage by artist Mary Maguire subtly signifies a sense of place, as do the hydrangeas and Nantucket roses freshly cut from my yard," says Bewkes. "Setting the table is my creative outlet and allows me to celebrate my passion for pattern, color, and artisanship without permanently affecting the décor. It is different almost every time, so I never get bored!"

Designed by Stacey Bewkes

In Charleston, designer Carolyne Roehm creates a deeply personal library that can double as a gathering place for a meal. "The idea for the 'dining room' was to *not* have one," explains Roehm. "I have always found that it remains underused. Its biggest function is as a walk-through space to get to the kitchen. This is why I always make the dining room a library. I work in this room all the time. I have a table that has drawers on one side. Sometimes I even paint in this room."

Designed by Carolyne Roehm

Below: The lighting fixture in designer Charlotte Barnes's dining room was never meant to be permanent. "I tried several lights here, but I couldn't land on the perfect one. I saw this basket in an antique center and made it into a light fixture, and it has remained," says Barnes. "I love how it brings a casual soft light to the room." She designed the chairs to be super comfortable, to encourage her guests to linger at the table.

Designed by Charlotte Barnes

For her Connecticut lake house, designer Tamara Meadow Bernstein uses sleek modern lines—like the glass-and-steel wall dividing the kitchen and living spaces—and captivating textures to create a space that both enhances its stunning lake views while rewarding its guests with interior ones.

Designed by Tamara Meadow Bernstein

In John and Rachel Robshaw's 19th-century New England cottage, cheerful patterns, colors, textures, and textiles transform the dining room into an exotic retreat. John used a staple gun to cover the walls in abaca fabric from the Philippines so that it could be easily removed when he got bored of it. A pair of Moroccan-style lighting fixtures furthers the mood.

Designed by John Robshaw

Above: Designed for warm and inviting evenings with friends involving endless conversation and multicourse meals, this dining room perched on Connecticut's Lake Waramaug is purposefully open and expansive. "I used my signature textured neutral palette and allowed only the organic colors of petrified wood to prevail," says Wendy King Philips, creative director of Interlude Home. "It's a calm, luxurious room that can accommodate a lively crowd."

Designed by Wendy King Philips

Opposite: Designer Christopher Howe knows how to make the most of a dining nook nestled in a corner of his weekend retreat in the English countryside—by combining casual yet unique furniture pieces so that the eye delights in the unexpected mix.

Designed by Christopher Howe

Kitchens

Every room in your home, no matter its function, should feel like it has soul, but the kitchen is generally considered the house's epicenter and magnet. No matter how much space you have, people will inevitably gather there. A successful kitchen—through its layout and personalization—makes you feel emotionally connected to the space and allows you to bring that feeling to your guests. Personal expressions in a kitchen shouldn't just be reserved for refrigerator magnets but can extend to the artwork on the walls, the color of the paint (goodbye cold, sterile white!), the lights above the island, the tiled backsplash, open or closed shelving, cabinetry, and so on, down to the pattern of your dishware.

- Top left: There's no reason your kitchen can't reflect the same personal style as the other rooms in the house. Here, the owners' favorite shade of green and a well-curated selection of art and *objets* lend personality to a functional space.

- Top right: Adding a favorite tile or wallpaper pattern, displaying favorite collections, and installing a unique light fixture ensures the kitchen feels as designed as the rest of your home.

- Bottom left: There are so many ways to display your serving items and other kitchen treasures. You can stick to a single color for your walls and shelves, and dinnerware, for a uniform light and airy feel.

- Bottom right: You can take a more eclectic approach, painting walls and shelves different colors and displaying a range of favorite decorative objects. You can even install wall sconces on either side of your sink for mood lighting.

Left: Elizabeth Georgantas wanted to retain the historical qualities of her home while updating it to reflect her family's way of life. "We knew we needed more space and more general light and openness," says the designer. The "square" created by the beams is the original home, so we extended what you see to the left of the beam where the sink is and removed an old laundry, bath, staircase, and the bedroom above to expose the roof beams of this extension on the home. I wanted the island to be large enough for cooking with my two daughters, hosting dinner parties, and even as a homework base during Covid. I went with a two-inch-thick honed piece of Carrara marble. It's a stainable Carrara, so it will age with the home and tell the story of our lives."

Designed by Elizabeth Georgantas, Georgantas Design & Development

Above: An antique green cupboard with a collection of blue-and-white export china is a wonderful focal point in Robb Nestor and William Reynolds's River Road Farm kitchen in Connecticut. "We loved the blue and green together," says Reynolds. "The lamps are made from old toile-painted canisters."

Designed by Robb Nestor and
William Reynolds

Opposite: "The most important room in any Tangier expat's home is the wet bar and pantry, so we wanted to make the most of it!" says former Manhattan resident Frank de Biasi. "Between the kitchen and dining room we fashioned the space so that you enter through a traditional moucharaby arch framed with handwoven Moroccan curtains. The coral-painted wall of shelves is used to display our growing collection of vintage Moroccan and European dishes."

Designed by Frank de Biasi and Gene Meyer

"We are huge fans of open shelving and glass-fronted fridges," says Ted Kennedy Watson. "It lets you see what you have, and it lets you visually enjoy your collections every time you enter the room. Green is a personal favorite of ours, so we use it every chance we can!"

Designed by Ted Kennedy Watson and Ted Sive

The pattern of Frank de Biasi and Gene Meyer's kitchen floor in Tangier is a mix of reclaimed marble and locally made zellige tiles. A pair of vintage English pendant lights, Maison Volevatch brass sink and fittings, and cabinet curtains in a vintage Malian fabric provide the finishing touches. "I love to cook, and I wanted a simple kitchen with a functional layout," says de Biasi. "We added a skylight, which thankfully brings in a lot of light."

Designed by Frank de Biasi and Gene Meyer

Above: The jet-black La Cornue stove in Caleb Anderson's Manhattan kitchen is a functional objet d'art positioned beneath the window. A handsome material combination—white diamond granite, hammered brass, ebonized oak—creates an unexpected urban mood with a nod toward the original 1920s design. A brass mobile from German workshop Lappalainen adds an element of whimsy and interest.

Designed by Caleb Anderson

Opposite: "As our kitchen is an open plan with a breakfast and lunch area, we wanted it to be as muted as possible," says Philip Vergeylen, co-owner of the iconic design studio Paolo Moschino. The duo combined pared-back cabinets in pale gray with the clean lines of white marble to enhance the space's chic calm.

Designed by Paolo Moschino and Philip Vergeylen

Displaying collections on open shelves tells a house's daily story while still keeping the kitchen feeling open and functional.

Designed by Michael DePerno and Andrew Fry

Opposite: For the utility room off his kitchen, designer Carlos Sánchez-García wanted to have a relaxed and practical look—so much so that he tucked a washing machine and dishwasher behind gingham curtains. "We keep lots of vases for flowers and jars for the preserves we make," says Sánchez-García. "To be able to view any ingredient at a glance without having to open endless doors was paramount." He painted the woodwork on the shelves, windows, and doors in the same color as the kitchen walls to unify both spaces. The gingham gives it an instant country feel, reminiscent of his beloved mother's kitchen.

Designed by Carlos Sánchez-García

Above: "I didn't want a pantry closet that was tucked away, but rather very much a daily part of the kitchen," says designer Elizabeth Georgantas. "While we were renovating, we found the most incredible library in an 1800s brownstone in Boston. I decided to repurpose it and had my carpenters retrofit it for my new pantry. We added a marble countertop, and here it all is: an extension of my 1700s kitchen—updated, reimagined, and re-created."

Designed by Elizabeth Georgantas, Georgantas Design & Development

Above: "When the owners of this Nantucket wharf cottage engaged us to help them with the project, their original thought was to paint the ceiling a solid white, but I thought otherwise," says designer William Richards. "To me, the original ceiling gave the house character and a sense of history. As we developed the design, the client became more and more enthusiastic about old New England decorative treatments like spattered floors and incorporating antique pieces that reflected the history of the island."

Designed by Gary McBournie and William Richards

Below: "As my kitchen is also my dining room, I felt that the cupboards around the sink should read as a dresser base," says designer Emma Burns of her retreat in the English countryside. "I painted the woodwork to look distressed and added a chunky timber work top. A collection of manganese delft tiles form both a backsplash and a backdrop to the collection of glazed storage jars and jugs." Three wall lights above the counter serve as task lighting but can be dimmed to create an atmospheric dinner party.

Designed by Emma Burns

Above: Ted Kennedy Watson and Ted Sive's Vashon Island beach house is compact on space but large on impact. The open shelves, which they use in each of their homes, are a design element they go to time and again. "It allows us to see just what we have on hand and what we need to stock up on," says Watson.

Designed by Ted Kennedy Watson and Ted Sive

Opposite: In her manor house in Oxfordshire, designer Bridget Elworthy turns a utilitarian space behind her farmhouse sink into a charming showcase for her varied colorful collections of cups, jugs, and cachepots.

Designed by Bridget Elworthy

Below: Designers and avid collectors Bruce Glickman and Wilson Henley turned a strip of wall next to their restored antique kitchen window into a petite gallery for some of their favorite original early-American silhouettes and prints. The mix of sizes and frame materials—gold leaf and wood—energizes a normally humdrum space.

Designed by Wilson Henley and Bruce Glickman

Opposite: Fashion designer Johnson Hartig designed his quirky Los Angeles kitchen with an abandon that feels joyful instead of dutiful. The backsplash is customized with his own bold-patterned Plates and Platters wallpaper for F. Schumacher. The dead space above the cabinets is utilized for a display of tall baskets in varying styles that add charm and texture—and provide extra storage in a pinch.

Designed by Johnson Hartig

Bedrooms

Bedrooms are a sanctuary, and that can take any form that's personal to you—whether it's full of serene solids or popped with pattern. Make space for your laptop if you want or maybe your beloved pet. It can be just as full of light and laughter as silence and solitude. Choose any color you love, even if it's white, on everything from walls to linens. As in any room in your home, the only "rule" is to fill it only with what you love *and* what you need. This room is your emotional touchstone at the start and the end of the day, so never compromise: Purchase the canopy bed you've always dreamed of; stack your bedside table a mile high with every book you've ever wanted to read; keep the floor clean and spare or install carpeting, or even just a small rug, whatever feels comfortable for your feet; take your grandmother's chandelier out of storage and hang it; invest in a dresser that makes your heart sing every time you reach for your favorite T-shirt; use the good, luxurious bed linens you usually save for guests. And, of course, treat yourself to a few fresh sprigs of your favorite flower on your nightstand, no matter the season. You deserve it.

◆ Top left: Various shades of green—from the mixed bed linens to the bright green–painted walls—are juxtaposed against crisp white to create a fresh and striking bedroom retreat.

◆ Top right: There is perhaps no bedroom element more romantic than a canopy bed. This one truly delivers on its promise, piled high with pillows, enveloped in fabric, and surrounded by elegant chintz curtains.

◆ Bottom left: This bedroom nook is cozy and chic, thanks to the uniform colors and stripe pattern. A pair of bookshelves ensure you have everything you need at your fingertips.

◆ Bottom right: A bedside table can be both functional and beautiful when you display necessary items alongside your favorite collections of treasures and art.

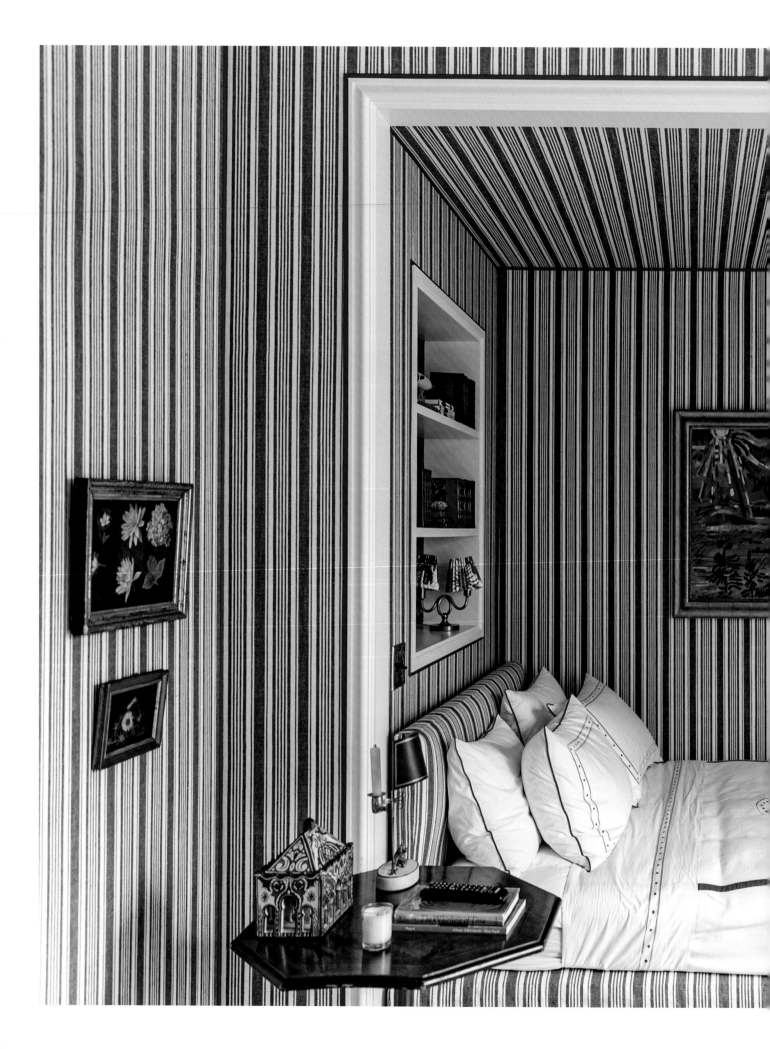

Page 184: Lulu Lytle's design for her daughter's bed came about because, according to the designer, she was "having nightmares after watching a rather vivid production of *The Lion, the Witch and the Wardrobe.*" Lytle explains her concept: "Pinning yards of fabric all around her bed to make her feel cocooned was surprisingly effective, and these scalloped bed curtains are a more permanent and all-enveloping version of the makeshift hangings. The bedcovers are always changing here, and most of my old Turkish and Greek fabrics look charming alongside them."

Designed by Lulu Lytle, Soane

Pages 188-189: Designer Katie Ridder and her husband, architect Peter Pennoyer, created a bedroom oozing chic coziness for their daughter, Gigi. They covered the entire nook using the same stripe pattern and then trimmed the space and linens in red. Built-in bookshelves create extra depth and storage.

Designed by Katie Ridder and Peter Pennoyer

Opposite: "The bedroom is an intimate space, and the objects should represent some of your most private and intimate interests, things that you have to explain to no one," says Karen Suen-Cooper. "The more honest you are about the objects that represent your interests, the more interesting your bedroom will be. As your interests shift, the objects will naturally change."

Designed by Karen Suen-Cooper and Martin Cooper for the Punctilious Mr. P's Place Card Co.

Opposite and below: Why save colors only for your linens? Color literally envelops designer Jeffrey Bilhuber's main bedroom from top to bottom. "There's a sense of anticipation about a bedroom," says Bilhuber. "Bedrooms in general need to reward those expectations with unexpected flashes of color and energy. A red bedroom is simultaneously regal and exhilarating. The flashes of sapphire-blue glass balance the glories of red-linen walls and act as a neutral to temper their boldness and confidence."

Designed by Jeffrey Bilhuber

For this guest bedroom overlooking their pool, Jeffry Weisman and Andrew Fisher chose a garden print from Clarence House in blue and white for the curtains framing the steel-sash French doors. The duo's Midas Two Tier chandelier adds to the light and bright feel of the room.

Designed by Andrew Fisher and Jeffry Weisman

Above: "I love mixing patterns in every room—I feel it gives a bit of personality and also makes a room feel cozy," says Charlotte Barnes. The designer does this to elegant effect in her guest room enriched with blue and yellow hues.

Designed by Charlotte Barnes

Opposite: "This bedside table in my New York apartment serves as media central," says designer Bunny Williams. "Phone, iPad, books, magazines, as well as a lacquer box to hold remotes, glasses, and things I love. A small drawing and two rock-crystal rabbits that my husband, John, gave me are also close by—and always, fresh flowers."

Designed by Bunny Williams

"This 'Tree of Life' fabric from Pierre Frey is one of my all-time favorites," says Mark D. Sikes of the pattern he used in his own Los Angeles home. "I fell in love with it when I first saw it in Givenchy's Le Jonchet. The pattern was the jumping-off point to the room, but I knew I wanted to layer in many other textiles to complement it. I also love the combination of blue and red: it's the perfect contrast."

Designed by Mark D. Sikes

Below: In the magical guest room of Veere Grenney's Tangier hideaway, the designer marries a sense of escapism with touches of exotic color and pattern, but grounds it all with a hushed sophistication.

Designed by Veere Grenney

Opposite: Repetition helps tremendously in all design, but even more so in a tight space. In this guest room, the oversize rectangular mirror over the bed reflects lots of light from the nearby window. More subtle rectangles and square shapes are repeated not only on the quilt but in the artwork hanging on the wall. "The quilt reminds us of Sister Parish and the dotted linens of Albert Hadley, which is why we are so fond of both of them," says owner Ted Kennedy Watson.

Designed by Ted Kennedy Watson and Ted Sive

"When decorating bedrooms, you really only get the walls and the bed, so I always try to make them interesting," says designer Miles Redd. "I never tire of chintz wallpaper, and who does not like to sleep in a garden? I also love canopy beds, as they can lend some drama and coziness—which are always pluses to me—especially in the bedroom."

Designed by Miles Redd

Bathrooms

Arguably, the downstairs guest bathroom is the most visited room in the house, just because of its proximity to living areas. And personal bathrooms play a vital role in how we begin and end our days. But regardless of who uses it, every bathroom in your house should be as beautiful as you can make it. Naturally, functionality is at the forefront, but the bathroom can be a good place to flex those design dreams you've been quietly harboring. Try that wallpaper you've always loved or that moody paint color that makes your heart skip a beat.

◆ Top left: Including a comfortable chair, a vanity, and art in your bathroom transforms it into a spalike haven.

◆ Top right: A stand-alone bathtub in a unique space is truly a luxury. And the vertical stripes of tiles create a fresh, modern look.

◆ Bottom left: Botanical prints covering the walls like wallpaper bring a lovely and serene unity to this powder room.

◆ Bottom right: Nautically themed towels and art impart color and personality, as well as a sense of place, to a small bathroom.

Page 204: For her Montecito, California, bathroom, designer Suzanne Rheinstein says, "I knew I wanted 'a tub with a view'—this looks out on my little walled garden of climbing roses and perennials. I furnished the simple room with some favorite painted furniture and treasured art. It's become a haven."

Designed by Suzanne Rheinstein

Opposite: For a guest bathroom, designer Penny Morrison picked a verdant wallpaper pattern (designed by her daughter Sarah Vanrenen, no less) that is both elegant and whimsical. "I wanted something striking and fresh," says Morrison. "The results are much loved and admired by everyone. Adding the pictures on top gives it substance and form."

Designed by Penny Morrison

Opposite: "We wanted to create a vintage look in our guest bath," says designer Wilson Henley. "And a powder room is a great place to have fun with artwork. Hang things you may feel don't go in your public spaces. Guests usually have time to take them in and comment."

Designed by Wilson Henley and Bruce Glickman

Above: The bath in Jeffry Weisman and Andrew Fisher's pool house has traditional Talavera tile walls in classic blue and white. Above the local limestone sink hangs a shell-encrusted antique mirror to which Fisher added a Moorish lattice.

Designed by Andrew Fisher and Jeffry Weisman

Opposite: In her house in Nantucket, floral artist and illustrator Cathy Graham mounted beautiful botanical prints in contiguous white frames to bring both unity and beauty to her powder room.

Designed by Cathy Graham

Page 214: In Andrew Fisher and Jeffry Weisman's home in Mexico, a powder room is transformed into a fantastical modern grotto, complete with mother-of-pearl shells encrusting the ceiling and walls covered in silver leaf. The panel is vintage 1940s Fortuny. The shell-encrusted mirror is by Fisher.

Designed by Andrew Fisher and Jeffry Weisman

Page 215: In his small Manhattan bathroom, designer Caleb Anderson chose luxurious materials—such as a vanity top paired with a Calacatta marble. "I look for stones that connect or complement in color and contrast through their movement or veining," says Anderson. "The materials are further connected through my choice of grout color on the walls."

Designed by Caleb Anderson

"One way to give bathrooms more personality is by balancing the presence of plumbing fixtures with furniture," says architect Gil Schafer. "If possible, I try to make bathrooms big enough to incorporate either a chair, to throw towels or a robe on, or an étagère for stacking magazines or books. Converting a piece of furniture into a sink stand is another way to make a bathroom feel less 'bathroom-y' and have more old-world character."

Designed by Gil Schafer

Below: Mixing beadboard—both thick and thin, horizontal and vertical—allows for lots of visual interest in a small space. The Americana theme comes through in the colors of the towels and table.

Designed by Ted Kennedy Watson and Ted Sive

Opposite: "I'm hoping this will encourage people to be fearless with color in the bathroom," says designer Penny Morrison of her guest bathroom in Wales. "I once saw an old bathroom in a large country house painted glossy like this and thought it looked so cool and simple. So I copied the color and added the bits—I didn't want it to look too modern."

Designed by Penny Morrison

Opposite: For a primary bath that had no windows, designers Andrew Fisher and Jeffry Weisman incorporated an oval brick *bóveda* (dome) with a vented glass skylight at the center and then added more over the sink, shower, and toilet areas. For a relatively small footprint, the bathroom is surprisingly spacious and bright. The floor tile pattern, traditionally used in single rows on stair risers, is turned vertically and doubled to create a pajama-stripe effect that feels both modern and traditional.

Designed by Andrew Fisher and Jeffry Weisman

Above: "I wanted to create a large family bathroom and not cut up the room into little bits, especially since my partner, Alastair, likes rooms to keep their architectural integrity," says designer Justin Van Breda of his retreat in the English countryside. "I made the most of the house's strong bones and then softened them, relaxing the space into a serene haven. The indulgence of a freestanding bath, lots of pillar candles, and the fabulous view out over the hills— it would have been wrong to add curtains because the window casements are so pretty—make it the most relaxing spot to have a long, lazy soak."

Designed by Justin Van Breda

Visual Landscapes

Whether along your mantel, bedside tables, library shelves, or even across your entryway, creating visual landscapes gives you a chance to relax and play. The masters of display know that it's not about showcasing a like-minded collection but rather knowing how to combine your pieces—old and new, expensive and sentimental—in a delicate dance of height, texture, and color. The only qualifier is to use what is personal—and what delights you.

- Top left: A richly layered vignette imparts beauty while also telling a story. Favorite objects and artworks from the owner's travels are arrayed on a green table and hung on a patterned wall, creating a visual feast.

- Top right: Curios from nature combine with family heirlooms to bring a delightful dimension to this elemental arrangement contained on an oval tray.

- Bottom left: It's all in the edit. This simple sculptural tablescape brings a sense of drama juxtaposed against the white wreath and pair of photographs on the wall behind.

- Bottom right: Creating a visual landscape on a radiator top makes incredible use of space. Here, curated treasures from the natural world are given structure by the framed artwork hanging above.

Page 222: A corner layered in pattern, artwork, and books becomes a chic cocoon for reading or contemplating in designer Miles Redd's Manhattan townhouse. Redd's own Cubist Silk Panel fabric for F. Schumacher on the chair anchors the space and draws your eye.

Designed by Miles Redd

Pages 226-227: Tastefully done, faux plants—no matter the season— are an ideal way to bring cheer and beauty to tablescapes in a vacation retreat that might not be used every day. Designer Ted Kennedy Watson's faux geranium on this desk filled with his favorite objects becomes a beguiling and unexpected accent.

Designed by Ted Kennedy Watson

Opposite: In Lulu Lytle's London den, the vivid presence of her green Rattan Leighton table complements the Soane's Lotus Palmette wallpaper in Raspberry. Lytle's collection of Islamic metalwork and paintings accumulated in her travels lives effortlessly among these bursts of color. The key, she says, is "to ensure it never feels too precious or unrelaxed."

Designed by Lulu Lytle, Soane

Opposite: This Spanish 18th-century table in the living room of designer Madeline Stuart's 1930s Santa Barbara cottage teems with character. To augment that, she artfully mixes equally exotic objects—like the Han dynasty urns—with a lush plant that lightens the vignette by bringing in a touch of the outdoors.

Designed by Madeline Stuart

Above: A grouping of small, precious objects in different textures and materials can make a big visual statement without a lot of fuss. Using a tray as a border, designer Mark Sikes creates a quiet tabletop moment for some of his favorite objects.

Designed by Mark D. Sikes

Designer John Derian's East Village apartment in Manhattan is outfitted as warmly and eclectically as his eponymous shop. The rough but simple vintage table is the perfect canvas for the assorted treasures on it and the elegantly arranged cluster of artwork hanging on the wall above it—proving that the only rule to displaying what you have is to display what you cherish most.

Designed by John Derian

Thoughtfully placing treasured objects from childhood among more grown-up sentiments is a great way to transform small spaces into intimate spaces with impact. "Common objects hold just as much value to me as an expensive treasure," says designer Schuyler Samperton, "which often leads to quirky tableaux filled with special postcards, meaningful rocks and shells, Indian textiles, papier-mâché boxes, and dogs in all forms."

Designed by Schuyler Samperton

Even a radiator surface can be used to create visual magic. Designers Susan and Will Brinson added a compelling wall color to what would normally be a forgotten area to create an expansive backdrop that showcases curated treasures in varying heights, all balanced by the level pair of framed pictures above.

Designed by Susan and Will Brinson

235

Above: Karen Suen-Cooper and Martin Cooper combined different natural elements to bring a delightful dimension and whimsy to this table vignette. The edited pieces exhibit their flair for the dramatic and romantic.

Designed by Karen Suen-Cooper and Martin Cooper for The Punctilious Mr. P's Place Card Co.

Opposite: A carefully arranged silver collection may glint and gleam in its polished glass home, but it doesn't necessarily encourage constant use and appreciation. Instead, designers Paolo Moschino and Philip Vergeylen have fun with their eclectic collection by not only housing it in a rustic case but also by displaying it in a whimsical, almost haphazard jumble that makes you want to grab for the soup tureen to use at every meal.

Designed by Paolo Moschino and Philip Vergeylen

Opposite: A fireplace mantel adds a whole other dimension to decorating. A landscape can be created not just horizontally, but above and below its border as well. Designer Miles Redd curates textures, shapes, and objects to create a moment of restrained visual interest around his Manhattan town-house fireplace.

Designed by Miles Redd

Below left: Arresting landscapes can start on tables and extend to walls. Wilson Henley and Bruce Glickman juxtapose a horn-framed mirror and 18th-century portraits with a bronze dog and glass hurricane lamps. It's all about how the balance of objects combines with the spontaneity of the surrounding textures.

Designed by Wilson Henley and Bruce Glickman

Below right: Repetition is a good tool to use when setting up a moment in your home. There is a monastic strength and beauty in celebrating just a few tones and textures. Designers Brooke and Steve Giannetti opted for a palette of restrained gold with one strong accent in this small bookshelf.

Designed by Brooke and Steve Giannetti, Giannetti Home

Pages 240-241: "We think it's important when designing and arranging a surface that you pay attention to highs and lows, positive and negative spaces," explains Wilson Henley, describing how he and his partner, Bruce Glickman, design in their home. For example, the large Robert Longo photographs, from his series "Men in the Cities," make a bold statement and actually provide a counterpoint of negative space to balance the more solid-feeling wooden console and the various objects deftly arranged on top.

Designed by Wilson Henley and Bruce Glickman

Opposite: "I love having something living on my mantel along with any objects I put there," says architect Gil Schafer. "Big branches in containers can be another way to bring the outdoors in and keep us connected to nature inside the house."

Designed by Gil Schafer

Above: Tucked in a corner of Miles Redd's Manhattan townhouse, this small tabletop bar makes space for an eclectic blend that meanders between objects large and small and drink accoutrements in all the best ways.

Designed by Miles Redd

Right: Creating a visual landscape doesn't have to be a serious undertaking. Known for infusing a sense of fun into her designs, Elizabeth Georgantas gets cheeky with her collection of vintage George Briard barware when outfitting a petite corner bar in her Nantucket house.

Designed by Elizabeth Georgantas, Georgantas Design & Development

Above: A bar area isn't only about offering a drink to your guests; it's also an opportunity to delight them with plants, art, and collections—all the things in your orbit that you love. On her own bar cart, designer Lulu Powers juxtaposes a vibrant pink orchid with a tray of small items to create a surprising personal moment.

Designed by Lulu Powers

Below: Bedside tables should never be just a place to keep a lamp, phone, and latest mystery novel. In his former Los Angeles home, Citrus House, designer Johnson Hartig, founder of the fashion line Libertine, made the most of the opportunity to express his creativity by gathering his beloved objects with a sense of highly edited spontaneity and whimsy.

Designed by Johnson Hartig

Opposite: Varying the length of open shelving is a great way to create openings in the wall to hang favorite frames or objects and also makes room for items of different heights. For these curated shelves made from old scaffolding in their Ojai, California, home, design duo Brooke and Steve Giannetti also kept to a neutral palette within two or three tones to heighten the cohesive effect.

Designed by Brooke and Steve Giannetti, Giannetti Home

Plant Life

Whether you live in a studio apartment in a
sprawling city or a house deep in the country,
surrounding yourself with nature is as imper-
ative to your well-being as the temperature in
your rooms and the food in your pantry. But
you don't need to have a green thumb to live
with green. It's as simple as treating yourself
to a small bouquet of flowers on your bedside
table or placing a pair of plants in pots in your
living room window. And remember that
containers can bring as much impact as a
blossom's color, so keep a variety at hand.
Even a simple branch or fern stem in a glass
vessel brings a singular beauty to your room
that rivals any precious human-made object.

◆ Top left: A single tall strand of greenery on a small corner table provides a simple and striking vignette.

◆ Top right: The power of pairs is on view here with potted ferns bringing a pleasing symmetry to the tablescape, echoing the plates arrayed on the table and wall.

◆ Bottom left: Using vegetables or fruits, rather than conventional flowers, makes for an unexpected and dramatic arrangement, and feels particularly apt as lunch table décor.

◆ Bottom right: A beautifully shaped plant in an antique container may be the only centerpiece you need for an elegant mantel display.

Page 248: A bouquet of flowers is sometimes only as good as the vase they are displayed in. Here, at Bridget Elworthy's Wardington Manor in Oxfordshire, a vintage, almost classical, urn perfectly captures the spirit of the entry's whimsical surroundings while elegantly elevating a free-wheeling arrangement of wildflowers from her garden.

Designed by Bridget Elworthy

Left: Plants can have an equal impact as part of the table setting when creating an enchanting garden dining room. In her Connecticut garden room, designer Bunny Williams places an abundance of low greenery on the table so it's at eye level with guests and not intrusive to the conversation.

Designed by Bunny Williams

Pages 254-255: Nothing feels more English country house than the stunning simplicity of masses of rambling geraniums in terracotta pots.

Designed by Sophie Conran

Below: "Many people like to use generic glass containers and buy expensive flowers to put in them," says designer Suzanne Rheinstein. "Through the years I've collected one-of-a-kind vessels, and I go in my garden or to the corner deli to gather humble branches and flowers."
Designed by Suzanne Rheinstein

Flowers correspond with their surroundings as much as any manmade object. Here a large bouquet seems to flirt with the mirror and a decorative bird in the nearby window.

Designed by Emma Burns

For the entry hall table of his Long Island, New York, country house, designer Jeffrey Bilhuber paired small and large pots of ferns with a neatly pleated table skirt in a profound Prussian blue. The combination brings a note of unexpected natural beauty and bridges the gap between indoors and outdoors.

Designed by Jeffrey Bilhuber

Above: "I'm by no means an expert flower arranger," says designer and architect Gil Schafer. "I just try to use the many things I picked up from my mother while she was alive. I like using two or three varieties at most, and very often only one. And I like arrangements that are a little imperfect, asymmetrical but balanced so that nothing feels too stiff."

Designed by Gil Schafer

Opposite: In his Los Angeles home, designer Mark D. Sikes illustrates how a potted plant in an elegant blue-and-white container can act like a perfect punctuation mark within a design vignette. It emphasizes a moment while asking us to pause.

Designed by Mark D. Sikes

Pages 262–263: Paolo Moschino and Philip Vergeylen's extraordinary collection of blue-and-white Tournal porcelain gets a prodigious pop of green from two oversize ferns.

Designed by Paolo Moschino and Philip Vergeylen

Opposite: Pairs of very different objects can bring balance and delight, especially when plants are included. On a side table, Jeffrey Bilhuber contrasts a duo of potted plants with a pair of plates hung on the wall and on the table to achieve a harmonious effect.

Designed by Jeffrey Bilhuber

Below: A bouquet of flowers is sometimes only as good as the vase they are displayed in. Here, at Bridget Elworthy's Wardington Manor in Oxfordshire, a vintage, almost classical, urn perfectly captures the spirit of the entry's whimsical surroundings while elegantly elevating a free-wheeling arrangement of wildflowers from her garden.

Designed by Bridget Elworthy

The addition of a live plant amidst collected treasures acts as a
wonderful punctuation in an assembled vignette.

Designed by Wilson Henley and Bruce Glickman

Sue and Will Brinson use the willowy balance of a fern to soften the more steadfast lineup of objects across their mantel.

Designed by Susan and Will Brinson

You don't need formal bouquets when guests
come for a summer lunch. As Jeffrey Bilhuber
demonstrates at his own table, tall stalks
of rhubarb and fern tendrils bring a casual,
unexpected beauty and are the perfect accompa-
niment to the menu and surrounding flora.

Designed by Jeffrey Bilhuber

Acknowledgments

This book would not be possible without Stacey Bewkes's amazing vision. From the moment she sets foot in a room she knows what is worth capturing and how to best remember it.

And, of course, thank you to all the inspiring and instructive designers who opened their doors to us.

As always, thanks to my amazing editor, Ellen Nidy, who makes the process an ease and joy.

And many thanks to my art director, Kayleigh Jankowski.

Opposite: "When we purchased the house, there was a circular driveway and several large blacktop parking areas just adjacent," says Gary McBournie of the Nantucket house he shares with William Richards. "Our desire was to separate the house and parking area with a courtyard-style garden. As the idea developed, we decided to encircle the area with a privet hedge and create more of a surprise or a secret garden via a wooden door painted in a nautical blue color. We also removed the glass from the panes in the top of the door, and small birds regularly perch there or simply fly through!"

Designed by Gary McBournie and William Richards

Photography Credits

All photographs are by Stacey Bewkes except:
Page 75: David Hillegas
Page 76: Alison Gootee
Pages 148-149: Romas Foord
Page 160: Federica Carlet

Above: In his own home, designer Juan Montoya proves that casual stacks of books can be a delightful way to beckon guests in to have a seat and explore his worldly collections.

Designed by Juan Montoya

First published in the United States of America in 2023 by Rizzoli International Publications, Inc.
300 Park Avenue South • New York, NY 10010
www.rizzoliusa.com

Copyright © 2023 Susanna Salk

Publisher: Charles Miers
Editor: Ellen Nidy
Design: CMYKayleigh
Production: Barbara Sadick
Managing Editor: Lynn Scrabis

2023 2024 2025 2026 / 10 9 8 7 6 5 4 3 2 1
ISBN: 978-0-8478-9907-4
Library of Congress Control Number: 2023967321
Printed in China

Visit us online: Facebook.com/RizzoliNewYork • Twitter: @Rizzoli_Books • Instagram.com/RizzoliBooks
Pinterest.com/RizzoliBooks • Youtube.com/user/RizzoliNY • Issuu.com/Rizzoli